PASSION
SEEDS

**Winner of the third
Vernice Quebodeaux "Pathways" Poetry Prize**

PASSION SEEDS

Suzanne Ondrus

FIRST EDITION

Little Red Tree Publishing, LLC,
635 Ocean Avenue, New London, CT 06320

Layout and Cover Design: Michael Linnard
Text in Minion Pro, Trajan Pro and Ariel.

First Edition, 2014, manufactured in USA
1 2 3 4 5 6 7 8 9 10 LSI 20 19 18 17 16 15 14

The photograph of Suzanne that appears on the back cover and page 128, taken by Raymond Di Carlo.

All previous publication credits of a number of poems in this collection are listed at the back of this book.

All photograph, other than the photo of Suzanne by Raymond Di Carlo, are in the public domain and illustrate various seed pods, shells and seeds.

The author and publisher gratefully acknowledge the copyright holders of the poem excerpts: Nizar Kabbani "Love Letters" from *Arabian Love Poems*; Hart Crane "My Grandmother's Love Letters" from *The Collected Works of Hart Crane* and Shireen Madon "No Fabliau for Love" from *The Journal 37.3* The publisher guarantees in good faith that serious efforts have been made to locate and contact the copyright holders to these poems. The publisher remains available to discuss the necessary permission for non-exclusive publishing rights usage.

Library of Congress Cataloging-in-Publication Data

Ondrus, Suzanne
  Passion Seeds / Suzanne Ondrus. -- 1st ed.
    p. cm.
  Includes index and notes
  ISBN 978-1-935656-27-2 (pbk. : alk. paper)
  I. Title.
  PS3612.A58565S77 2014
  811'.6--dc23
                                        2014012001

Little Red Tree Publishing LLC
635 Ocean Avenue,
New London Connecticut 06320
www.littleredtree.com

CONTENTS

III

IV

V

VI

ACKNOWLEDGEMENTS

Thanks to mentors Larissa Szporluk, Amy Newman, Penelope Pelizzon, Christian Doumet, Jean Hubert Bazie, Sharona Muir, Maria Mazzotti Gillan, Sean Forbes, and Liz Rosenberg.

Gratitude to Major Jackson for his *American Poetry* article calling for hearing the racist voice in poetry; your article gave me the courage to write from the darkness.

Thanks to fellow poets: Melissa Parker Helton, Stephanie King Strickland, Nick Strickland, Byron Kanoti, Tasha Fouts, Dan Rzicznek, Matt McBride, Jeannie Kidera, Gary McDowell, Julie Platt, Michael Cherry, Erika Lundbom, and Hilda Twongyeirwe. Thanks to editors John Galletta and Jim Pavlish.

Hugs to my encouraging friends Dianne Ritchey, Florence Bacabac, Margret Katwesige, Hilda Twongierwe, and family Mary Ann Leonard, Christina Ondrus, John Hogan and Ray Di Carlo. Special thanks to Adam Spells, without your kick in the butt this book would not be out in the world! Lastly, recognition to those passed: Ruth Stone, Tom Ondrus, and Ruth & Louis Goldbach.

INTRODUCTION

You have before you a handful of poetry seeds in Suzanne Ondrus' debut collection aptly titled *Passion Seeds*. These poems speak to both what we want to keep invisible, such as shame and racism and speak to what we want visible, desire and love. I recall how in a birthday greeting to William Meredith, Hillary Clinton defined poetry and poets as "our purveyors of insight and culture, our eyes and ears who silence the white noise around us, and express the very heart of what connects us, plagues us, and makes us fully human." It is this ability a poet has for translating the world for us that is perhaps his greatest value, his greatest gift. Here Ondrus translates an interracial and intercultural love story. Poetry enables us to see the world anew like Gulliver returning from his journey to find his homeland totally the same and totally new. Poetry at its best describes a new human paradigm for how we interact with the world, even how we love. And the method is not rational. It is the work of a shaman who connects seemingly antithetical threads of reality into the cloth of life. The dream-world is where ingenuity lies, for both poets and others. Einstein, it is said, discovered his theory of relativity in a dream and despite this highly abstract and counter intuitive formula, it is the "reality" that enables us to create nuclear energy as well as the atom bomb. Ondrus taps into both the dream world and reality so that the invisible becomes visible and audible.

The introductory poem "Invisible Offerings" of Suzanne Ondrus' *Passion Seeds* could serve as a metaphor for the poet's ability to present the reality that stands behind reality:

> crack the shelter,
> break the seed's shell,
> so promises green,
> becoming
> visible.

What are the dreams and future promises she reveals to us? And how does she conjure the seeds to grow?

Passion Seeds is a story of longing and desire, elements essential in erotic work. Ondrus' mysterious poem "This Circular Space" speaks to how the erotic, like a seed, is present in us. She says to her lover:

> Before you
> there was a fold
> inside me,
>
> The pulse, the inner drums, were silent to the world.

He responds:

> *I need your combustion, the fireflies you bring*
> *from Ohio. I will call them into me*
> *and let them glow*
> *for all my nights.*

And by the end of the poem, they have

> gifted flowers
> and fireflies
> for the red cave.

How right the fireflies image seems for physical desire and the tenderness suggested by the illumination created between two lovers. Desire has moved from a "fold within" to a "red cave" and then blossomed into a flower. Indeed, it is love that changes us, and a good poem also changes us. This brings to mind Shelly's comment that in reading, "We murder to dissect". Well, a good poem, like a field of fireflies, can illuminate many associations and is an interactive exercise as unique as the reader.

As per the title of this remarkable work, often the poems take the vegetable world as inspiration. Ondrus contemplates how love "seeds bring invisible to visible." The plant realm is one place where this love story unfolds. In "Fully Colored Green" the poet is actually overtaken by plant life, "vines intertwine" with her veins and her "joints flowers bloom." Tendrils fill her cells with oxygen, such that she rises like a balloon to "expand and expand" as love does for us. The plant realm morphs from the outside world into the domestic sphere, where in "FruitLove" she ponders the enigma of a kiss, who's giving, who's taking that sweet pleasure:

> Dear, are not both our mouths
> on the same piece of fruit, pulling
> towards something we cannot see,
> only feel?

And she moves to the financial realm to consider if the two could find their

>   ...gold
> in mangos—

Another seed that takes root and flourishes in this collection includes Ondrus' preoccupation with black magic. She is sometimes at the mercy of such magic and other times, a practitioner. In "Expelling Love," a private ritual frees her from

>   ...that external power—
> that black tornado whipping you
> 'round and 'round,
> always bending your spine
> back to his voice.

The details of this practice are exotic and inviting. Like pulling petals from a Daisy to know if she is loved, one ritual involves spinning a burnt match "to know your love's heart." Another from "The Evil Face," requires that she check the color of menstrual blood daily:

> Redder: listen close. Brown: ask for attraction to freedom.
> Know the magic in yourself. Draw on it at the full moon
> with arms raised high, silently split your loaves of bread.
> Save the heel to etch out undesired results.

Dabbling in Black Magic can be a double-edged sword, however. In "Stages of Paranoia and Sincerity," she recognizes that her beloved is enslaving her with voodoo love potions but finally accepts their power:

If my boyfriend uses voodoo on my heart, well I know he
        loves me,
because I require a lot of spells and sacrifices. I am one high
        maintenance voodoo chick.
How many times after I tell him, "No, I'm not happy. We need
        some time apart." does he
throw the chicken bones, peacock feathers and his own hair
        before the crocodiles? And I
come back, re-instated with love, with desire, waiting for his
        smile and bird dialogue.

Suffice it to say there are sufficient "real toads" in Ondrus' "imaginary garden" to qualify as one of Marianne Moore's "literalist of the imagination." Many of the poems will raise the hair at the back of a reader's neck. Others call for quiet contemplation, such as the one about global warming where she declares "It's hot in here brother, open the window, breathe." On describing the desire for a child, the earlier inner fold and red cave become the flowering of love, "an inner ache" that pulls to dreams of a future child, "soft, small, helpless and fighting in … [her] arms."

Through many of the poems we trace the history of transcontinental desire from Burkina Faso, to Benin, to Russia, to Ohio. Her lover is black and if anyone believes we live in a post-racial world, these poems will dispel that notion. Ondrus shows how racism and prejudice are some of our invisible seeds. Poet Martha Collins asks: "Don't we have stereotypes that if one is in an interracial relationship then one automatically has no racism, as if it evaporates?" Ondrus' work bravely examines how it is indeed hard to erase racism from one's self, a theme rarely addressed in contemporary poetry. In "Black and White Love Play," the epithets hurled at the interracial couple by the imaginary audience during their lovemaking cannot be silenced; the voyeurs cannot be sent from their room. Still, there is hope. With love "vibrating silently" in her bones, even geography seems to be pushing for resolution to the pilgrim's quest, where as the African tectonic plate pushes up the European plate, and Mount Triglav rises higher (a nod to the poet's Slovenian heritage), slowly but surely these two organic worlds merge. Her "Valentine's Day Card 2007" attests that:

Today I am your swan,
my thighs, white wings,
cradle and enfold your molasses
torso that drips thick over me,
making sugar in my marrow.

As the poet urges following one's heart, even if it means transcending racism, she also speaks to a world where one is free to travel anywhere. In a short poem entitled "Air," she expresses her longing to go where the wind goes, as

free movement
with no passports
and with no boundaries

though she does not know where that may be. One recalls the divine loneliness other pilgrims have described in another context, where the invisible becomes sustenance.

Love and desire become an invisible power that can transcend the space between America and Burkina Faso. In "Missing You in Herb Garden" she wants:

to quickly
arrive
at you,
to exhale over continents
and heave the Atlantic's waves

In this respect perhaps, like all really fine poets, Suzanne Ondrus speaks for us all.

Richard Harteis
West Palm Beach
March, 2014

Pour Camille Narelwindé Badini

Maam nã kete n nõnga fo

My letters to you
transcend me . . . and transcend you
because the light is
    more important than the lamp,
the poem more important than the notebook,
the kiss more important than the lips.
My letters to you
are more important than you
    more important than me
they are the only documents
in which others shall discover your beauty
and my madness.

-Nizar Qabbani, "Love Letters"

"There are no stars tonight
But those of memory."

-Hart Crane, "My Grandmother's Love Letters"

"Who we need we shed our skins for,…"

-Shireen Madon, "No Fabliau for Love"

I

Invisible Offerings

Seeds bring invisible
to visible.
They shelter dark shining.

In this world,
letters pressed on paper
push permanence,
as if small strokes of ink
could dominate fields
of white.

Lovers propose,
but God doles.

Letters travel
the Atlantic,
just folded paper,
with flat consonants
and vowels,
but inside lavender honey
and roasted goat meat
drip under a balafon's
vibration.

The right conditions make dreams,
crack the shelter,
break the seed's shell,
so promises green,
becoming
visible.

FruitLove

Yesterday a mere mango glaze gloomed
me, parting at the airport.
Today, in Ohio, I smiled at mango sorbet,
you sweet in my heart;
spoon by spoon the sorbet wooed,
from Ohio to you
in Burkina.

Today I wonder what is in your mouth.
I wonder why your mangos are so sweet,
sweeter than the Philippines
or California ones.
            The soil does something.
I ask today could we find our gold
in mangos--
in the erotic fruit men speak of
when they want a woman who is so ripe
they could pluck her from the tree?
Could mangoes build our home?
Pesticide free, they would yield
quite a profit here.

Liberty and money are sweet.
Dear, are not both our mouths
on the same piece of fruit, pulling
towards something we cannot see,
only feel?

Seeds of Love

Deep in our personal soil, planted
and watered by nymphs behind the sun
are the seeds of love.

While we sleep they mix the seeds up
and we watch what grows.
This is the origins of love potions.

Love then makes its rounds,
driving forward,
cradling us in its elliptical arms
till we can walk.

       My mind on an unnamed country.

       Bronze calling.

       A man waiting.

Orange puddles reflect
yellow and green trees,
while vultures' glares
separate the visible
strong embrace.

A distant country speaking
through the years,
calling forward through lines and
lines of writing,
to where I could firmly unfurl,
held with its red soil, its tam tams,
calabash, and backwards steps
from graves.

Behind the sun my seeds of love
chant and carry me forward
to coat my feet red and fill
the circle, solid.

This Circular Space

Before I arrived
you never reached
for flowers.
Before you
there was a fold
inside me.

The pulse, the inner drums, were silent to the world.

It was a crumpling, a falling, you came
to me one wet evening and said *hold me*
I am cold, I am cold here in my Africa.
I need your combustion, the fireflies you bring
from Ohio. I will call them into myself
and let them glow
for all my nights.

You asked me to take your hand
and reach for the descending
flower over our heads.

We stretched ourselves
along the bark,
gifted flowers
and fireflies
for the red cave.

Self Possession

In the equatorial sun my shadow
was burned. I learned to laugh
at myself,
riding 'round the karate tree,
speeding away from the small squealing monkey
that gnashed the green fruits
and spat them at the wheels
ripping by.

I continued on the circular path
at the base of the tree.

In my memory freedom is:

in the sounds between me and the monkey,
in the death of the eaten fruit,
in the way the soil rose up
as the wheels turned over and over.

I Carried You Before You Fully Came

in a folded chocolate wrapper,
underneath smooth belly skin,
in pimpled face, with empty sighs
yearning for hope, in an inner ache
pulling you towards me—there were
the startings of you. And I dreamed
of you soft, small, helpless and fighting
in my arms.

Fully Colored Green

Vines intertwine
around my veins and
in my joints flowers bloom.

You are deep
in my vitals—
a special mineral
polishing leaves
and glistening berries.

You twist tendrils into
my tiniest cells,
clearing dead matter.
I expand and expand;
the air overtakes me.

Look, I am rising!

The Light of Your Father's Love

Your father comes burning through your smile,
wide as the fields at dawn where your small hand
grasped the pick ax. Tall and proud now, he shines out
from your fearless eyes searching the plain, scattering flecks
of light on your future path. Shoulders wide and strong,
he sits upon you light as the sun,
burning through your erect frame,
radiating out from your chest.

You light your way through the air,
solid and dignified,
striding with all his illuminated particles
beaming you a self-possessed man.

Bleached History

I.

White through fire circles,
mud houses, lingering handshakes
white through indigo, slit goats' necks
and the dolo-filled calabash.

II.

A congregation so large,
piled high up to the sky
for only one step to his throne,
to finally come home.

III.

Missionaries pleaded, cajoled
for their congregation to reach that throne!
They even stole boys to enroll
and control,
promising parents future rewards.
Their heads were shaved
and their mother tongues shamed,
with the antelope skull worn at least
once by all.
Cultural carving beyond bones,
branding
Jean,
Marc,
Antoine
over Narelwindé's
wings
to God,
on top *Awa's whisper*
to the river
and Yalle's *hope risen.*

IV.

The red soil with its orange puddles
held this pain,
so full from
what the whites called religious school.

They tried to stitch boys against the hum
of their ancestors in the wind,
and with white cloth, bread and wine
wind their minds for Christendom and
the French curriculum.

But whispers of songs
sung in the field,
lingering handshakes,
compounds with family
and thatched roofs commanded feet
home, through thorned brush

stealthy under the moon,
back close to Mother's womb
from where solid like the baobab
they did first bloom.

In My Blood I Carry You

The accordion strikes chords
of my ancestry.
I normally do not listen to it,
but tonight polka is on the local
radio, on the Slovenian hour,
and I've nothing better to do
than cook and listen.

The accordion sound urges my feet to hop,
though I stand still stirring cookie dough.
Polka is an idea pulsating in my veins,
lighter than the Slovenian sausage, *potica, krofe,*
and *flancate* circulating in my blood,
ladening it with dangerous fat.

The accordion invokes Lake Bled's
white church on a small isle.
The note of pilgrimage,
pristine pilgrimage from Cleveland to Slovenia,
from the sixth most polluted town in America
to a country capped by the Alps,
snow rimmed even in summer,
vibrates silently in my bones.

I want to see this country that still grows vertically,
reaching new heights year by year
thanks to the African tectonic plate pushing
it up, so Mount Triglav raises herself
higher slowly but surely, like how cookie dough,
eaten raw spikes my blood sugar and raises my lips
to smile at this Slovenian polka
sound on a lone
Saturday night.

Global Warming and Internal Combustion

It's thick wood
cinder blocks and hot stones
begging for water,
one ladle-full, to explode vapor
into air, to make colorless color hang for ingestion
into cells, so they can purify, so they can push the beating out—
for moisture to meet moisture—sweat to steam—steam
to sweat. And isn't that sometimes just what the world is,
a hot room enclosed into itself?

Blood flows but words are sparse.

Our world erupts through airlets
in the sky, asks for a cold-water bath to purify,
close pores, seal mouths and shut eyes.
It's time to jump into ice, snow.
Time to seal and rinse, cooling (hot heads).

We make saunas everyday,
but don't listen, just spew.
It's hot in here brother,
open the window—breathe.

Speak Loud, Listen Great

When I can't move that's when my arms rise
and I ask for light. I need to know how to speak
how to echo, because I am not alone here. There are

piles and piles of stones. And rivers full of crawlers.
I pinch myself to open up to the present,
the cherries hanging heavy in July, yet it's in the blur
of swirled paint, the unfocus, that the peripheries widen
and influx is received. Speak to solitude, breathe widely.
Cry echo cry.

It's a fistful of walnuts, a crouching close to earth,
that asks us for our voice, for a slow walk,
our touch on the land spreading to footprints.

You meet me in the light, face the cherry pickers
and fall into the basket whole, resonant,
cradled with humanity.

You touch me to know the texture of other skins,
to break the form, to peel back the seven layers
and mend somewhere deep inside the echo—

Scratching Back

Weeks ago it must have been,
I don't remember what or where.
We were somewhere,
You grabbed my hand
 And you said:
"It must go like this."
And I pulled back,
a little lighter.

Something scratched.
Some mark was left,
like a dog sniffing dry leaves.

> I am a white woman.
> I am silent when stolen from.
> I fumble, saying *"Bonjour"* instead of *"Bonsoir."*
> I smile widely at strangers on the street.

I don't remember what or where, but
I came to this red land for you.
I came for a dream.
I came because of a feeling.

I wanted the sun of Africa to shine on
me. Now my dream, my feeling—
they are moving with the Harmattan,
scattered beyond sight, impossible
to even touch.

And all I have is dry air and dry air,
and I don't know about its duration.
I don't know when love will return.

Perhaps it'll be in the living room,
with your griot shouting praises on tape.
You'll swing your hips and shake,
bending your knees,

and it will begin to rain—
to push through the shutters
and flood under the door,
wetting your moving
bare feet.

II

Voyage for Hope

The young man seeks the voodoo man's eyes for a promise.
He wants to make her gaze
long at him, hear her soft coo
while he moves his arm to pull her in.
One whisper, one kiss, her long gaze, make it mine.
the young man wants this dream,
so he steps up to the open door, smiles
at the voodoo man holding a palm-full of blue feathers
over a low flame on the floor. He almost whispers
the words magic and victory.
He rests his forehead on the doorframe, inhaling deeply with hope;
he's brought what's needed: photograph,
dirt she walked on, strands of her hair,
and piece of her clothing, unwashed.
The young man shifts his weight, watches
the current customer on his knees kiss
the voodoo man's feet, gather some of the feathers
and exit.

She knows her cure, the young man waits for his.

Expelling Love

Spin one acorn, still green,
under a kitchen table at midnight.
In the hollow of the floor it will stop;
this is your special spot. Place
one bright copper penny face up
on top. Blow three times over it
towards West. You should feel
a shudder—so sudden—shake your soul.
Stunned, you won't want to move. But rise;
get off your knees and rise; turn three times
clockwise with arms crossed
over your heart, then leave immediately.
Smile, you're standing straight for yourself.
Now you're free from that external power--
that black tornado whipping you
'round and 'round,
always bending your spine
back to his voice.
You control your will now,
hard
and
fast.

Fierce Love

It's gardens of rose petals blasting.
It's a million tamtams
pounding.
It's a flurry of razors
flying into flesh.
It's a thousand
and a thousand
baobabs breaking
through the soil.

It's an ion here
and there
whirling,
spinning,
shifting
to

recognition.

The Space Between

In the orange sanddorn berry clasped
tight to its crown, long before that gap,
ever so miniscule appears for separation,
  Like one's timid smile with a hair's space of air--
The space between:
  Rome and Catania
The moon and earth
Blades of grass—
I pick it up to fill some distant emptiness between
my eyes and heart.
I run from its expansion,
fearing the stretch, fearing expelling.
  The oily wool gathers in my head,
all soft and dense
till hardly any air is left.

  Wait, I wait for—the statues don't even know.

It's here in the kinks,
of each strand, ingested
and brought to light to touch.

  Make me shadow invisible to touch.
  Make me pewter, reflective

so I can receive the shine of a brow and smile
reflecting light.
Spin the wool inside Grandfather,
  spin in front of your sandstone
  fireplace early in the morning.
Take the space between—from nothing
  to something—a ball of yarn waiting
for the loom and the wooden shuttle.
  Open me up,
pinch and pull, pinch
and pull, winding my way to completion.

Compulsion

My lips pull
on a mango pit in Benin while my mind traces
an orange sea buckthorn studded coast to Russia.
Here in Africa I assemble rolling Russian pomegranate seeds.
The white chalk cliffs pierce the rosehips
by the Baltic Sea, reigning in the rolling
juicy kernels sold from the mittenless babushkas hawking at Metro stations.
To step into another skin is why I travel.
The unfolded land, opening then dropping,
holds me with the whistle of the train to Nizhniy Novogorod.
In this dry land, with mango in my mouth, raspberries and beets rupture
into shreds of clothing against pines while the train went by,
the torn uniform and the prior impact of iron against flesh
still moist years later. Death tore through me and I cannot walk away.
Wet cobblestones and blue clay deepen my foothold.
But, I am here in Africa to reach upwards,
through dangling mimosa flowers' yellow, white and purple,
and scowling vultures. Over this red soil a whistle, a tatter,
a speaking. A crackling comes over the land's sweep, traveling
the Atlantic. Under the karite's green flesh the watchman's core
flashes by while his ribboned flesh hangs in the pines. My eyes close
over his turned body. I hear the gravel roll while the birch trees snap.
I heard a language that I still hear, how moving, motion can lead to an end,
how compulsion is death. How inside the fruit there is the fall—
motion's cessation,
my vertical growth.

Inside a Kiss

I.

By stretching we welcome,
        braiding out filaments of air
for one another to enter
and mend our halves.

II.

We moisten onyx silk
        for the exchange of jewels,
kernels and husks.

III.

I present my pieces:
        shoulders, elbows and wrists,
to you my burned black African
whose name means
        wings to God.

IV.

You regard me,
        and kneel down slowly
to part the pomegranate.
        Both halves in one palm,
their craniums shining at each other,
you dig under the white membrane
and collect the reddest pearls
to rub over my parted lips.

V.

I haul buckets of coal out
from my innermost depths,
light them and blow the hot glow
towards you.

VI.

With one bronze-coated exhale
your elephants' tusks embrace me
            and arch over my extended hands;
I am living in the ivory ring,
enthralled, whole and wild.
            I wander with the antelope at dawn.

VII.

My crystal gazebo shatters
and instead of shards of glass,
snow falls all around.

My amber boat bubbles
back to thick pine tar,
with beetles, spiders and stones.

VIII.

From these worlds we breathe.

IX.

We fall whole,
            spinning down
a tiger-maple staircase.
            Hands spread
scattering gold,
your mouth open wide
                  spiraling down
inside mine.

Evaporation/Absorption

In midsummer it came with red soil.
I was open all at once.
The red clay with its iron filled me.
The mango trees blossomed,
and the rains fell creating orange
puddles in seconds. Evaporation,
absorption occurred.
While the sun burned cement blocks,
I made two seeds
but ate one. One is waiting;
with time it will find the soil,
the rain, the tender sun.

In a measure of flour
we share a humble meal.
With plates we know division.
All of our stomachs 'round
the table. In memory we divide
land, state, language.
You open your mouth to speak
but sound doesn't swell forth—
instead salt and sand spew out.
Winds reign between us now,
and we are silent,
not sharing air,
water or land.

There's a space between us
filled with many people's voices,
jumping spiders, unripe apples,
crackling and spitting wood.
Divisions come,
widening the air between,
pushing us apart.
It's the tension
of separation
that splits

and snaps.
It's silence,
deadest wood,
that severs
easily.

Ascension

I.

Between jumps
      over crossed sticks
jumps on numbered
chalked squares
and runs along the compound's walls

they turned,
      spinning their names:

Narelwindé and Awa,

as vortexes
      propelling:

Valerie, Fabian

like white tissue paper

into the wind.

II.

Memory still walks.

The orange puddles still speak
rattling *français, français*
      against the antelope skull.

It's a cruel world.
      Nature cannot help.

For each turn
many years come undone.

      Speak indigo.

Speak fire.

       Cry dirt, cry.

III.

Carry me home.

Open my mouth
       and coax the mud out,
to spill over my lips
and run down
       my chest.

Mam yeeta Kongossi,

My back is cowry shells.
       I leap to Wuro's voice.
       I am sun on Earth.
       I am a shaking furry spirit

leaping to perfection
       head high.
I am wind.
I am soil.

IV.

       My arms stretch
I crack the Baobab leaves,

       harvesting history.

This heartbeat of mine, of ancestors, shouts,
reigns over—
my sealed seed.

This rhythm from within

       chants my history.

Turn, turn,

      I am wind
I am soil,
        Arms to Wuro
Turn, turn

Mam yoor la Narelwindé

A Single Breath

In the heartbeat a stop occurs, so sudden, so quick.
You can only make a few good mistakes in this life.
Somewhere in the black hole up there light opens.
I want to tell you something.
In a dream I knew your hand, much more than in reality.
Save me, carry me were my words.
Some mistakes last a lifetime, like that macheted flesh melting into flames,
turned up to the clouds and back to beyond.
Somewhere there was a hum, giving my heart extra beats,
the strength to clasp tighter and to feel every fold of your skin.
When we carry a life inside there is extra air.
We must mean what we say, for in this life there is no other.
Carry me, save me were my words.
If you can speak, somewhere your sputterings are weaving with stars,
far beyond our eyes.

III

Air

Sometimes I wonder where the wind goes,
and I want to go too,
even though I don't know where.
I want to be sound.
I want to be free movement,
with no passports
and no boundaries.

By the Fire

Narelwindé: Love in her eyes. Please, m'ba.

Medicine Man: Kneel down beside me.

Narelwindé: Her forehead on my shoulder.

Medicine Man: Open your hands. The falling and the cry are the same.

Narelwindé: Her whisper, her kiss, her long gaze!

Medicine Man: Give me your shadow. Open your hands.
(Places blue feathers over the fire)

Narelwindé: Make her heart mine. Please. (Presents the woman's photo)

Medicine Man: Good, her photo in color. (Narelwindé presents a small folded piece of clothing. Medicine Man sniffs it.) Her scent in fabric, good.

Narelwindé: Please.

Medicine Man: You must open, really open those hands wide…

Narelwindé: Her hair, lifting in the wind…I will step whole into the fire.

Medicine Man: Sid'sida? Your will is strong.

Narelwindé: (slumps) My voice has left me. My shadow has pinned me.

Medicine Man: (becomes angry and gesticulates) What? A thousand goat sacrifices could not take you, but a woman! Shake, shake her power out! You must stomp and stomp. Do you understand? Hair or no hair, if Zizi has gotten inside…

Narelwindé: Her forehead, her smile… I need her for my own life. (gazes down at the fire)

Medicine Man: (scowls) The soil, the wind, rain and sun have been inside you for years, years before her...

Narelwindé: Victory, magic... spell them in the ashes, please!

Medicine Man: (puts a cowrie shell in his mouth and hums) Na dee raa, na dee ra

Narelwindé: Draw her arms tight around my waist again.

Medicine Man: Push away your shadow. Orange over black, the fire is pushing, pushing. Her feet will be fixed, trust me. Do not fear. I have power beyond your eyes.

Narelwindé: Rooted so she won't move?

Medicine Man: She won't budge for hyenas or crocodiles.

Narelwindé: (implores with eyes) Please.

Medicine Man: But you on the horizon, will cause every sinew in her to twitch. Trust me. I have wound all your cares and exploded them far far above our heads.

Into Separation

It was in November,
the middle time,
when deer seek fallen apples.
Our bushel had fallen.
You wanted to heave it up.
I told you leave it
by the wayside.

       A raven watched
       as we parted.

You know this road we cleared does not continue.

I ask you for forgiveness.
I ask even though
I might not receive.

       Blackberries still hang
       in the forest alongside pines.
       In the meadow
       thistles are trampled
       and the birch bark
       is peeling.
       These are the signs,
       in black and white,
       masculine
       and feminine.

I'm sorry to share them, but forgiveness for life
and living cannot be asked.
We parted and it's best we continue.

When the fog comes
it will touch our shoulders.
I am wrapped in frost.

From Africa to Russia

It's time to go back to Russia,
where I can pack myself with boiled *pelmeni*
those bundles of pork and chicken,
where I can smear gobs of Siberian white honey
over my sauna reddened skin,
sink myself into a *vatrushka's* cheese center,
and stare hours through snow
at the pretty, red place,
winding my eyes up to St. Basil's
golden dome.

It's time to go back to Russia with heartbreak,
back for solidification, mending, filling.
Where shall I place him this time?
In a troika, in a samovar,
in a loom or among the wild pack
of dogs gathered outside the metro?

Mangy, un-groomed, listless the dogs lay,
waiting for kindness—
a dropped chicken bone, a *pirozhki's* end
or a greasy napkin.
It's here I place him,
out in the open, where everyone
passes by.

But it would be dangerous.
He'd likely be pummeled
for being black.
And his beautiful wide nose
would be smashed.
His hair in clumps on the concrete
and his thick soft lips
cracked, pouring forth no words,
but color—red, red, red.

And I wish I could have understood him better,
grasped the drawn out A's
of his *Mooré* language and poured
beautiful paragraphs into his ears.
But something wasn't there,
and so among the mango,
karate and nere trees I couldn't stay.
I cannot spell it.
There were too few deep wells
between us—and humans are 90% water.
And camels can only store water
for a specified number of days.

The cowrie shells had to be spoken.
They spelled come undone.

Descending

Here in the reflection of snow I flow
down stream, one with Mother Russia.
Obliteration of self,
that's what it's called.
Dispersion of me into trees, air,
water. The disintegration of me
line by line,
cell by cell,
flaking off to get to something white
or red that moves out and retracts,
in unison,
in quick movement,
with no saunters or turns,
just jump out
and jump back,
true to itself, with nothing left
to flake off, just raw with the air.
In direct contact pushing and
retracting from---

It's brimming, needing to drop.
When I'll drop, I'll fall,
        fall into a deep ravine
where among stone I'll rest, resonating
deep within the earth, tumultuous,
free with stopped motion.
        It's here that I wish to end--
in the Cuyahoga Valley,
where clear massive weights
once moved, scraping,
leaving something permanent.
Something touchable. It's here,
the indentations. Pulsing.
My hands grasp stone
through moss, fall into
the scraping, the cutting.
One time, forever moving
with permanent marks.

To Know It's Over

Each photo,
Each you,
Shifts of eyes, of lips--

Only photos of you penetrate,
Only photos of you feel like layers,
Only photos of you touch me so,
Only photos of you make me feel
Like I can step inside the person,
Can feel what the photo portrays.

Only photos of you pierce through me.
In each photo of you I can see a different you;
I know a different you.
Maybe this is what love is, knowing.
I didn't know at the time of the photos
That what I was capturing was love.

They say you only know how much you loved something once
You lose it. I've lost you now. I still feel your photos.
I didn't know that I knew you.
I knew you.
I felt you through my spine when we danced.
When I look at photos of you I feel you through my hair,

Skin, arteries, organs and blood.
Once you told me Tu es dans mon sangue, you are in my blood.
I did not know then the significance.
How could something like that come so quick?
But now I know. *Tu es dans mon sangue.*
I dance with you buried deep inside, flowing
Through me. I saw you and I could not walk away.

But if I do not see you, do not look at your photo,
You are still in my blood, coursing through my veins.
My response, my knowledge, to your photos shows me I loved.

But the question is your present photos. Maybe I would say no,
I don't know you.

Maybe those photos would remain on the surface, glossing by,
Me oblivious to your mind at that time,
Not knowing the weight of that smile,
The push upwards of the light in those eyes.
I knew you intimately once.
I loved you once.
But presently we are separated,
Separated by land, by ocean, by time, by career goals,
By some greater calling, by family,

And I cannot feel your depths in your current photo;
It's all veneer, veneer that won't crack,
Hardened by my departure, by my "no."
Hardened by fear, by obstacles, by visible barriers.

I am here and your photos are in my drawer.
Every time I look at them I still feel those layers;
The past cannot be erased.
I cannot pretend I didn't love you. I still feel that love
When I look at the past.

IV

You Don't Always Get What You See

Today I dreamed you burned
yourself white for me.
Chunks of flesh were gone
from your forearms.
Your flesh burned white,
holed with red craters.

Today I wanted you black.
There could be no other you.
Today I filled your arms' missing
flesh with my hazel eyes.
You said "it will heal and still be white."
My eyes filled.

Gone was your face as I knew it.
Before me was a man afraid.
Before me your soul journeyed out,
and I couldn't smile anymore looking
at you.

Whiteness brought sadness.

And I was alone
in a car barreling up a hill
through rain and darkness.
Look forward.
Look forward.
        Have faith.
        Have faith.
He'll follow.
He'll follow.

Let's Go Green

Dante had Beatrice blazing blond before him
guiding him from the ice of hell to heaven's
summits.

Beatrice burned forever in his heart.
Her hands filled with air
and her smile shouldered the world.
From afar he would watch,
happy for a view of her on Sunday.
In the Duomo, his heart arched over
the bridge his eyes made to her,

silent,
unaware
he prayed.

My black angel, you are afar.
How shall I say you burn for me?
My love for you glows like coal or
you are my black angel of coal glow?
But you are not coal, licorice, chocolate,
tar, oil, rubber, sod, tires, or asphalt.
You are seed in my heart,
          the green promise.
I want to be the seed of your heart;
I believe I am the seed of your heart.
Please water me with your tears
and bring your heart to the light
so our seeds can grow and glow green.

If a Sudden Shadow

The trees and sandstone are gone.
Our conversation's gone, sliding
under water in a big slow shadow.
Yet we still pulse out, our hands grab
and grasp. Inside there is darkness,
so I keep my mouth shut.

Black plastic covers it all—
the park bench, hills and trees.
We are pulled down under water.
Your hand has slipped from mine.
But in the darkness there is clarity.
Nothing but a gasp, a stretching
for the light.
        And this sole man
        sitting by his fire drum
        smoking a fish,
        warming
        his hands.
Peeled under we sink.
There is stillness of the body.
Flashes speak an inner fire
that our eyes no longer can.
I hold my breath and wait.

Always on Stage

Together we are actors
in one body:
black body
with white arms and legs.
But even alone with you,
in the most private room,
I see them in the mirror:
spectators staring
at my hands clenching your dark
shoulders. They shudder
as my hands cup your buttocks.
They whisper, *It's just jungle fever.*
While I rub the back of your head,
they grimace and draw back,
exclaiming *nappy hair.*
They then push in against the mosquito
netting, poking your flesh,
poking mine. Their words wind around
my throat. I close my eyes, nestle my nose
into your neck and take your scent,
that's like rubber,
deep into my lungs.
You are comfort.
I touch your chest and feel the need to rub
to the muscle, to the bone,
but they press against the netting,
and I can't send them from our room.
The words wind around my throat
jungle fever
nappy hair
rubber
as they cajole and poke.
Then your chin starts to arc,
from my nose to my forehead.
And I want to see this.

Your mouth opens,
your eyes close and press tight,
and then your cry comes.
I smile and kiss your cheek,
pressing deep into your high
cheekbones, finding my own skull.

Seven Yesterday's and Today's

Yesterday I cradled coconuts.
Today the Harmattan sprayed everything red.

Today is a fine day.
Yesterday the dog shat outside my window.

Yesterday a truck filled with coal tumbled.
Today cornmeal ground round and round.

Today you cannot see the sky.
Yesterday something inside me fell.

Yesterday a child was lowered into the ground.
Today I see Baobab leaves shine.

Today my basket is half full.
Yesterday a princess waited up the hill.

Yesterday chickens were out in the street.
Today a cry came and I held it tight.

Clarification

In a bank in Africa
with polished floors
elevators and air conditioning,
I'm asked how I find it here.
Hard I reply.
Hard, I continually see hands out
When I go by,
Hey white, give me a pen
No pen?
Give me your watch
Hard.
They see me as a bank
because I'm white.
This man, this African
banker, surprises me.
Our problem is we need to learn to give.
To give, Africa give.
He's the only one to ever say this to me.
Africa needs to give.
And I hear from other volunteers
how the locals will not volunteer,
For them it's all about money.
No pay, no do.
But what right do I
have to say hunger,
poverty is
their problem?

Plucking Inside

I called your scent "rubber,"
like tires.
I took your warm scent
from the recess of your arms
      and capped it to wheel rims,
      something that touches dirt
      on vehicles that move people
      so that they don't have to move themselves.

And I loved you, as much as I knew how,
with a mixture of tree gum
and the pulsing hidden in my cortex:
      This man isn't man.
      Black is separate.
      White is right.
      Black and white cannot unite.
      When blacks go with whites they climb high,
      and when whites writhe with blacks they seep low.

      Oh, I loved you so tight.
I wound around you like a tire to its rim.
When you were away my smile dimmed.
But how did that word
      zoom out of my mind with fondness?
Did fondness really push that word
out of my heart
to talk about you?

I want the reason to be family,
some shading in my past
where Uncle said *we kept*
      our streets real clean with a smile,
      and I was silent,
as if this could not, did not, infiltrate me,
but there it is:
      His scent like rubber,
                  the image of Sambo grinning

red rubber lips,
      large white teeth,
                and black, black skin shining
                like shoe
     polish, like lumps of coal,
               like capitalistic endeavors and mines
For our humanity to pile and pile ourselves up and up,
      solid on the skulls
of others, ultimately the skin of no consequence:
      red, yellow, white or black.

Because our sense of stability matters,
the feeling of solidity, or of feeling certain.
        Oh I loved you so tight.
I was the shining
white angel
in your dreams,

               sent to rescue

    with money,
       blue passport,
           and promise.
I played that role,
        took it for all it was worth,
              elevated to some balcony
beyond reach. I loved you so tight,
      wound myself around your thigh
and cried "drive on,"
      holding the skin of right.

Happy Valentine's Day 2007

Today I am your swan,
my thighs, white wings,
cradle and enfold your molasses
torso that drips thick over me,
sugaring my marrow.

Muddy Love

I want to share with you my nature,
my temptations.
I want to share with you what makes my eyes run,
how I gather my tears and what I weave deep
into the base of my heart. I want to share
my inflated nature, my self serving self
that draws time out on the couch.
I want to spell l-o-v-e in algae,
fish eggs and radiator fluid.
I want to get messy
in this thing called life,
up to our knees in its putrid stench,
not floating on helium, but grounded,
sunk straight into quicksand
holding hands
trying to lift our legs.

Kneel Down

I've built a cathedral,
pearled, bone ridden.
This is where whispers crack and gasps land.
Stop. Put your ear here.
This temple feeds our breath.
Under the walls fine carmine cords
map this permanent cupola,
anointing and framing our hosannas.
Our ecstatic arcs of praise are
sealed in these warm marble walls
where you feel not the weight of the world.
Together we gather here to reach
the falling light. Together we breathe
jasmine vines, honey dew,
black pearls, ochre snow
and thousands of little tendrils
fluttering.

Where Roses Climb

For the water and sugar of the Burkinabe mangoes

The gasping, everything stopped. Sugar.
Press, press, press.
In the hollow
there's your whisper,
rounding out.
In the break
there's a room,
but no one hears,
no one receives my pulses,
my spasms.
No one absorbs my moans.
These three oranges.
Wrinkled finger.
Making the tender flesh contract and burn
for your wet black back,
rising higher than the foam
that caresses my hair in the tub,
That presses into and in_____
The hollow, rounding out.
There's your whisper—
My thighs squeeze.
How I desire to hold you close.
How I desire to receive.
Instead I hold a small basket
of wildflowers in my hand.

V

Clear Panes: A Family Affair

It's building a whirling in me.
He's at the table, eating
with my mother.
Black tulip buds streak purple
and pulsate.
It's tearing,
wearing the sheet thin.
The rotation builds--
laughter behind closed doors.
Spin, cut to
a lull in conversation.
The unopened black tulips
bleed out
across white fields.
Now a purple shadow descends
and the windows open
for a cold wind.
It's building a whirling
in me. Cut to three black
tulips spreading, ascending towards
the first one. It pulls
them through layers.
One bleeds brown and the other red.
Together they merge.
It's the end of the day.

The Evil Face

You'll see it hanging in front of you one night.
It will wake you up, fluorescent green flames flickering
behind its eyes. One single face. You will sit up
in bed and know strong fear. This is stage one. Beware.

At the next significant stage you will find clumps of hair.
Beware. At this point you are losing awareness of time.
Carefully count your conversation and composition minutes.
Tell him when topics are concluded. Write his name on a white
index card, fold it two times and put it in a box under your bed.
Be sure to untangle your hair every day.

Slow progression is the key to freedom.
In the waking moments it is best to avoid fantasies,
these further the voodoo love power. Hum a classical tune
and jump right in the shower. No dawdling or courage
will be lost. I never said this was easy.

When it's your period you have exceptional power.
Take this to your advantage. Steep in your strength.
Find assertive words that map your territory.
Check the color of your blood daily.
Redder: listen close. Brown: ask for attraction to freedom.
Know the magic in yourself. Draw on it at the full moon
with arms raised high, silently cut your loaves of bread.
Save the heel to etch out any returning flames.

Blood Connections

We three pick together
blackberries
under a poison-ivied
willow.
While we take sweet berries
into our mouths,
my Father's words about us
in the psychologist's room echo:

"They're like a yoke around my neck."

His face was red then.

We were silent,
waiting for the white walls to absorb
his thick hands
and straining red face.

He chose the word yoke
for us.
The message: burden.
Thorns came between us,
like how he had pressed the yoke
to my Mother one night,
blamed her for his unhappiness.

His hands wrapped around
her neck.
He squeezed and pushed
blood
up into her face.

Later blue bruises covered her.

Plump berries fall off easily,
full of ripeness.

My Mother did not fall easily;
she stood firm
and filed reports,
had photos taken.

My Father's rage rose,
at being forced to live away
from home.

We the family
were a yoke
pressing blood up
into his face,
pushing him
to burst.

My Father's thorns were hatred
for my face
that was like my Mother's.
He wanted to press her
from me,
but her blood will flow
forever in my veins.

My hatred was my Father's
red face and curled lips,
his squeezed fists.

Unified by a task,
we're together now.
While our hands claim
berries,
thorns claim
our blood.

We pick berries to fill
something.
We pick for sweetness,
for that which is not
in us.

Laceration Prayer

I.

It hovers in my lungs,
Pure crystal,
Creates termites from dust.

It's my self upon the stage
That must know
The glinter, the rise.

For time comes, on prairies
Waiting for a water drop.
I steep

For prayers unanswered,
For fields of crows to circle
And descend while the shaking

The shaking is forever
In the present,
Pushing cells.

II.

And you call out my name
In three-quarter time.
Where I can run I no longer know.

And if I knew would the beating stop?
On and on I push,
To reach the depth of raisins' creases.

Tulips in the spring, rain falling in warmth,
It hovers in me,
Around the inner lacerations, warm

And steeps sweat up
Gathered in bales, presented
To the new moon with exhaustion.

III.

If I sit in church will the steeple
Enter me? Climbing light
To the heart in perfect union?

If I sit at midnight
Beneath the yellow moon
Will deer come feeding?

Deer, white horses
Stampeding
Into my mind, and

Grinding down outer skin.
I am here, my hair comes loose
And I cry.

For the falling, for the mansions,
The treasures dust-clothed,
Waiting near windows.

IV.

To feed the fire one needs hard wood.
To feed the fire lacerations
Must be received with open arms.

I hear a gunshot tonight
And fall inside to the rusty
Staircase, dwindling.

We venture only so far until
White horses stop us—reach
The green grass and push

Us down, into the molten core
Where reversals pull,
Hum under stars.

IV.

Gold triangle wise
With one blue eye
See our blood flowing and hearts stopping.

Raise the deer, raise the white horse
And walk beneath exertion
Subordinate to life above.

Wait. It doesn't end here.
The deer call, running in the pine.
White tails fanned forward,

Faster, faster to the finish
What finish? It rises, spirals,
Resonates. Turns inside, yet

Its yet, turns individual churches
For unique Gods.
Foam-frost meets fingers

So we must separate,
Separate and divide to see
Where crows knock and preaching

Begins. To pull, to receive
These are the larger issues in life.
I see the fire burning beneath the beach.

It's small, a grass fire over
Remains. The ants walk away
To find the solace they know—

Building empires sure to fall.
The process, the unities calm.
It's a full moon tonight. The deer,

The white horse, call us to pray
Where truth is found, in ashes.
Gather carefully with both hands.

Potion in the Invisible Arrows

Blow gently, like an early summer breeze,
like into a baby's ear—so light—
patient for the drying, the hardening
of blood to their shiny cartilage points.
Stitch them into your shirt,
around your heart in a rectangle.
They will shift her mind to you. Patient,
just wear, wait and see.

It's Hard to Embrace Betrayal

Ouidah is where we spoke and divided.
It's where steps pushed between us
and an ocean
flooded in.
The Portuguese fort, this shell, was of my design.
How I adored the two curving staircases,
saw them as outstretched arms
saying welcome home.
The fort's inner balconies were like crowns—
there was no function,
only beauty in design;
this was my culture speaking.
How I had missed the familiar.
Part of me smiled.
I was in awe of a shell,
in awe of something beautiful
that did evil.

To you rows and rows of bound,
stolen lives spoke—
your blood, lives sold.
The white walls pressed tight
on your throat,
with men forced to their knees
to receive the iron-brand.
Burnt flesh singed your lungs
and the shackles tore
down to your bone.

We stood together but were alone
with anger in between.
For a moment I inhaled
while you gasped.
How could people sell people?
How could people buy people?
Black and white both guilty.
The shell as shell pretty.
The shell as shell evil.

I was there to hear your tears,
stopping you still.
You were alone, but I was
at your side.
Standing on-site you saw the peopled-lines
beaten forward into the holds,
felt every foot pound the ground
as they went 'round three times
the tree
of return,
praying for their spirits to come back
to their land,
their place.

We took a photo under the arch
of the point of no return.
Our hands squeezed
while our eyes squinted
and sweat ran.
We held tight for the shot,
the ocean pulling behind us.

The Structure Inside

It pushes in me to still the rising quakes and shakes.
There's a dove that asks for a little nest,
to see the heart encased with matches.
You fall to enter the abandoned barn,
to feed the stalled horses.
Together we pull full bales of hay
while the whirling saw rotates
through conquered fibers.
You ask me to tell you about Iran.
Sand covers my eyes,
and a scorpion pricks my toe.
You seek, you die.
Sand doesn't produce soft,
but wears down.
The dove stirs in the hay bale,
and a new moon is in your brown eyes.
Whisper to still the stalled
horses. Sit firmly while stirrups
sway, too long for your feet.

Spinning to Know

To know your love's heart
spin one un-burnt,
red-tipped match at midnight.

A.
If it falls to the West—
own interest at heart, best to move on.
Why climb a thorny rose-weed wall?

B.
To the North, maybe he'll turn
from his trail and join you on yours.
It depends on his reserves.

C.
To the South, he's definitely burning
his own fields and not open to carrying
any water with you. His pack is just
too heavy.

D.
And to the East—he wants to enter
your country, but stands scared
before the gate. Give him a smile.
You can speak from your heart.
He will listen; he'll be careful
with those tattered lace fringed
blankets you carry around.

Stages of Paranoia or Sincerity?

Suspicions

My boyfriend is enslaving me with voodoo love potions.

I know this is true.

After having written a five-paragraph letter on my grievances,
after his face has faded,
and I am ready to leave him,
I then wake up the next morning with a desire for his warm lips.
Desire too strongly brewed.

Voodoo love potions can travel the Atlantic

though I don't see how that butchered chicken's head can fly—
but voodoo love potions can travel.
Burned mashed spiders,
remnants of my hair,
chicken bones, an infant's urine
and one peacock's feather infuse
in smoke to keep me gazing
at this African man's photo
night after night.

Voodoo love potion is a real thing.

Every time I try to get up to go
I am pulled and tethered back,
staring into his wide smile,
pausing on his full cheeks.

That tuft of hair I left in my trash was fatal.
I know it sounds incredible, but I did think
about taking it with me, packing the knotted hair
in a plastic bag and just stuffing it in my suitcase.
Instead, I threw in the trash,
called it powerless and left.

Directly Addressing the Black Magic

That tuft of hair left in that white plastic bag
nests on the top of my brain.
I wonder if your fingers found it,
pulled it all up
and took it to your shelf.
I wonder how you ration it out, one strand, half a strand for each—
I wonder if you've combed it out to make a doll?
Certainly there's a full head of hair for a little doll.
I wonder if you wind it around your fingers
while praying in front of a candle.
Voodoo love potions are a real thing.
      People often marry for them.
How many strands were in that tuft?
      How long will they draw me back?

Resignation

If my boyfriend uses voodoo on my heart, well I know he loves me,
because I require a lot of spells and sacrifices. I'm one high mainte-
nance voodoo chick. How many times after I tell him "No, I'm not
happy. We need some time apart." does he throw the chicken bones,
peacock feathers and his own hair before the crocodiles? And I
come back, reinstated with love, with desire, waiting for his smile
and bird dialogue.

VI

Blackberry Babies

was the name
for shame,
for something so ripe that hung
itself in the grabbing.
The baby bump
from humping
before taking any vows
or signing any sheets.
Blackberry babies was the name
used to frame coitus' illegal results
with race to its name,
as if only blacks would grab
for something so ripe.

Controlling Sacrifices

In fifteen minutes we were smoke,
burned to the sky.
She said my ego was too high.
She left me.
I cry every night.

So brother, wash these beasts
slow, use fresh water,
the white towels and
new talcum powder.
Bring out the dove,
rooster
and goat.
Wash these beasts slow,
so clean.
This ceremony must go right.
It can't get any worse.
I'm tattered,
a frayed white flag in the wind.

I'm taking possession as best I can.
Give me the calabash, the knife.
One cross,
a plate full of millet.
Yes that's right.
Eat for my love!
Eat for her smile,
her footsteps near,
her lips on
my lips,
her soft words
in my ear.

Come goat, kneel
before Loba,
raise your head high.
In the name of Venus,

Aphrodite,
I ask you to die.
Bleed to fill
my soul.
This is for my future flesh.
This is so she returns.
Bring fire and candles.
Create an altar
to raise our love
high.

Wishing for the Void

My prayers are for a hollow,
for space devoid of things,
like an empty chocolate box,
the remnants of you,
of us, our love.
I want the air
inside the ribcage.
It's all I can grab for now,
and it's sufficient to satisfy.

Moving On

I still think of you daily,
five years later.
Although our ties have been cut,
our love remains like a tree stump.
This doesn't change the present,
the future.
Our tree will never make fruit,
will never flower forward.
Severed, the stump remains
long after its trunk has disappeared.
Humans with a severed limb
still feel it, call it the phantom limb.
Stumps take years, decades to decay,
their root systems wide, deep,
but life can sprout up, take hold
in the space between.
I try to keep opening,
letting light and air
in, around
your spaces, praying for our decay.

Post Holiday

Although the photographs of you are packed away,
Valentine's Day still gets to me.

It's a week after the holiday of love.
It's five years since I've seen you,

But you are fervently on my mind,
Not like desire or thirsty yearning

More like anger at the past,
Stumbling into a new room and

Not finding the walls to my height.
A problem solved.

Somewhere you are and
Somehow I want to know what you are,
When you do what you do.

It's just a holiday trigger.
Luckily there's a barrier to just reaching out
And dialing—I have no phone card,

And I can't remember how I used to get them.
So I sit and wonder

Thinking how and where you might be
Tonight under the moon,

The moon that never made us together,
But kept me yearning forward

For something still brighter
Than that stellar light
On a silent night.

This is My Vessel

I dream of building, doves
against peacocks, coated in red soil,
wrapped in bolts of blue linen,
and drizzled with hot tar.

This is my vessel.

My sound culminates
in doves stretching
their wings,
peacocks fanning their tails
and linen falling
in thick folds.

VII

Because Bones are Solid, Permanent

I call you into the ash circle
wanting honesty, forgiveness.
Sit. Across from me.
Close.
Squeeze your fear tight,
so tight your courage wins
and you can only speak the truth.
I am flush with the fire.
I've chosen to plant my legs here,
even to the point of my flesh melting,
leaving nothing but my skeleton
Because with the weight of boulders
I want to be so close to you
no air can come between
nor grain of sand
And this is why I need to hear the truth
even if it's betrayal and deceit.

Inch by Inch, Row by Row

Today you took your pen up for me.
The birds have begun to sing in January.

Tomorrow your smile will last seven seconds longer.
The bulbs will push up another quarter of an inch.

Yesterday you ate cookies from the capital city.
At midnight the fire broke from the basement to the attic.

Today I took you back into my heart.
The birds are silent.

Tomorrow I will sink a little back into myself.
And the bulbs will push up another quarter of an inch.

Yesterday I ate kale, celery, apples and pineapple pureed.
The fire-smell smoldered the air.

Today you ran forward against the rain.
The soup was thick with yams.

Tomorrow you will have to repress your smile for serious impressions.
There will be something sounding silently causing you to look.

Yesterday you went for your brother's life-model.
The gossip in the neighborhood was thick like a pack of dogs.

Today I breathe better with my heart open to you.
The ground is soft beneath the snow.

Yesterday I stood where slaves cowered.
An elderly woman's collie danced on a picnic table, chained.

Tomorrow I will step forward, worrying less.
And the bulbs will push up another quarter of an inch forward.

Fury Seeds

I want to pull you
inside, from over the Atlantic,
to unfold spinal cords,
and open fused eyes.
I want to know
all the little hands,
that will pull
the red wagon.
I want to know what
stirs one cell,
what cracks the egg's wall
open?
Whisper to me these secrets.

Tell me why wild horses are on
the beach,
why we like to see ourselves
replicated,
and bring the answers to me on a platter,
with fish and asparagus.
How long will your smile last?
How long will we hold each other?
How many will we place around
our table? I look up to the sky,
cock my head as if waiting for something
to fall. This could be the moment,
the moment I wait for in my sleep
when another heart has erupted
under my own skin.
This is prayer.
This is truth.

Dirt was never so welcome
as now.
We want the same soil.
We want to hold the same land,
reach from the same

footing. Even spit won't reach.
It's too good to be true. If a cloud can
cross the ocean why can't I?
Why can't I somersault in that invisible to
visible space at night? Why can't I fold my hands
over your back? Why can't I speak in dream,
and open myself for you,
for our future?

There's a black space at night, devoid of you
where I speak English,
dream English. There's no fire,
no street filled with motorcycles.
Instead a giant vulture
comes to my head—its tri-shaped nest.

This is fact. This is part of love.
What we cannot ask we cannot know.
I turn to you with eyes open and
ask, why don't I dream of you—
the one love?

           ~

      When I've found you
      among the yellow roses
      and taken all of you,
      then you'll know
      the satisfaction of having really eaten.

           ~

My love, inside there are seeds,
fury seeds with white wings,
your name tattooed on each and every one.
It's only a question of wind.
Bend down close, whisper into my ear.

In a million whispers one wind lives,
caresses one seed's wings to arc
back and collapse forward,
like a dying swan—
exhausted from a thundering bliss.

Our gifts come to us in destruction.

In the light
reflections live, pass to us
and live. I want to divide
out of reach. I want
your hand and tufted hair.

Missing You in Herb Garden

Crouching under the sun, parts of me tumble
on thyme spreading over slate.
I gather myself in the closed pink flowers
on one stalk of lemon thyme.
I am feeling the morning glories nestle
into the white barn's gutter,
and I want to pull you towards me,
with bee's wings, horses' braided tails
and dry maple leaves. I want to quickly
arrive
at you,
to exhale over continents
and heave the Atlantic's waves.
I bend close to the earth and hear
stars falling inside—
a billion minuscule mirrors fictioning
forward light,
transferring the invisible to visible.
I wait for your whisper.

Answering

Above a puddle,
behind the bus stop, steam floats.
I go to it, to ask myself if I can live
on your red soil for my life.

There's something I need to know—
How one creeps out for the offerings
at the crossroads.
How large quantities of water evaporate.
How my feelings for you manifest
and what I can hold in my hand,
when you're holding my hand.

I know only so much.
I must remain open
and continue to fill.
Will you wait for my return?
Will your hands remain outstretched?

In a dream you whispered stay here,
Je veux que tu restes avec moi—
The primal cooing,
to remain in the dark,
in the cave, us alone
against the fire,
our backs touching,
warming what the fire cannot.

Waiting in the Sun

Tips of wheat sway,
dripping over fields,
while gentle rocking
has been withheld
from my arms.
And I'm offered tea, hot tea
as if the stagnation of the sun
wasn't enough.

I lift the bag and it drips
red, then diffuses.
I want it to explode
and burn my failure,
to brim full
with blood.

I sit and wait in the heat
for time to pass,
for your small hand one day to pull
at my skirt. I sit for a push in me
to come, a push to lift my face
into a happy state.
I pray for the descending wisteria
vines from the pergola over my head
to wrap me, squeeze me tight
like the tea bag's string wound
over the filled little bag,
and soon I'd be taken away,
the dripping, the sliding, gone.

Because

you don't tell me
how my eyes
are like sunflowers,
how my hands are
like Boticelli's
Madonna's,
I sit folded
waiting. Some
blue and black shroud
shuts me down.
Will you graze
my cheek?
Will you speak it?
Will you do it?
I sit nights
grinding
and grinding
these white truths.
I sit reading
my frustration
waiting for---
what failed,
what fails.
This whip,
I hold under
my arm,
I don't even
want to see
if it's
still firm.

"Viens, Viens, Viens Chez Moi"

I wanted to be
that whisper
forever drawing
in your ear
tomorrow
tomorrow
more
and
more.

I wanted to be
that light
pulling
your lips
high
and
wide.

I wanted to be
what you would
push
and
push
forward
forever for,
through pits,
angry stares,
starvation,
narrow corridors,
and the desolate
wide open plain.

I wanted my body
to be what you wanted
to push and push into,

instead your words

entered deeper than you,
"*Tes fesses*
sont comme le mur,"
my buns
like cardboard--
I wasn't, wasn't round
enough,
but in my mind
          my buns
     were cantaloupes,
burning in your squeezing
hands.   My image sounded
louder over and over in my
mind. It streamed juice and
pushed seeds, pouring over
flesh, While your cliché fell

flat,

limp.

Distillation

If we could get to the essence of things,
like find what makes the sea buckthorn's tang
by pulling the berry's fibers and pulp,
would we find the color that makes fire?
Would there be some relief in knowing,
in holding an answer?

In me you turn my love.
I try to close my eyes, but you are there.
You are even in my breath.
I try to push you away,
try to extract you, but cannot.
The sweetness cannot be taken from the sea buckthorn;
it is sweet and tang together.

I was once your focus, but now feel pale.
Speak to me my love.
Tell me lies if you like, but speak to me.
I need to hear you love me with salt.

I lit a candle for us in Treviso.
Will you place a plate of bread
at the crossroads for our days
under the karate tree,
for our kola nuts and honey?

I dream of Africa at night,
when I am alone and pretend to sleep.
I dream red soil.
I feel soil coating the gossiping voices.
I see our hands together at night,
while our hips lightly shift
to your father's music.

I tell myself there is an Africa.
I tell myself once I knew an African,
a land, a man; I felt him through my spine.

There was a man who held me
with open eyes.
In his gaze I wanted to stay
with nothing else.

The Fear

Holds me inside
Restrains me
Makes me refrain
Drives me insane

The fear
Girds me
Keeps up
What I know
And keeps out
The unknown
So all I can see
Is up, up, up
And not out
Out, out.

Of Significance

Today we finally talked about it,
that event years ago, the shame
over my love
and affection for you.

I had snubbed you as I got off the bus
that held my fellow Americans.
I walked right past you without
a glance, without a handshake.
In that moment I cared more
about what others might think
than what I or you felt.

We had never talked about it.
I simply went inside the house,
you went inside the house,
and we took our time alone.

But all day I had longed
for seeing you waiting
for me at the front gate.
How I looked forward
to getting off the bus,
smiling into your smiling
eyes
and touching
your hand.

That day I took pleasure
away from myself,
away from you,
and I gave it to fear.

Months later this fear
was still there.
I kept you hidden,
your photo was out

only for my eyes.
Your name spoken
only to select few.

I imagined their revulsion
at your kinky hair,
big lips and flared nose,
yet your lips, skin and nose
I loved. If I could take just one
it would be your nose,
with its nostrils wide enough
for baby snails. Oh,
I could stroke it
for hours.

And where others
might just think black,
I saw a cinnamon face,
licorice shin scars,
carbon hair,
sandstone palms
and pepper freckles.

Shame is dangerous,
like salt on soil,
preventing
growth.

I need to claim this soil,
protect and respect
its sacredness.
I need a snake's silent
flicker of a forked tongue
to keep our border,
so what is between us
can reflect the sun,
can grow.

VIII

Contemplating the Reunification Ceremony

Shall we make our circle half of sandstone
and half of cowrie shells?
How shall we arrange them?
Half of the circle with your shells
and half with my stones,
or shall we intersperse them?
What words will you bring?
What cloth will I hold?
Will there be tears?
Will there be blood?
Will we make our love solid
like the Baobab and Oak?
Will we be soft like shea butter
and olive oil?
Will we be fierce with our own selves
as the hyena, the coyote?
Will we light our interiors so bright
that we will see nothing but days and days?

Fruit Withheld

Grandfather, I didn't give you any blackberries this year.
I withheld them for myself.
The plump ones went right into my mouth.
Oh, if I could so easily punish you—

for all the thorns you pushed in, that I can't extract,
even while I'm entwined in my lover's black arms.
Now don't go falling in love with any darkies.
They all hang full with juice.
It's too late. My hands are purple and I'm leaping
from sugar highs.
A pierce, a pinch—
Whatever you do, don't come back with a black husband,
and here I am two years with dark glistening.

I want to poke up through the snow,
unfurl my leaves and bear black fruit.
But there are thorns, even inside of me.
Aren't those nigger babies cute?
She lightened up and you can't even tell.
When girls go with blacks, they let themselves go.
And so the berries hang, from their little crowns,
and so it hangs, like thorns over lunch:
Ruth had a cousin once,
married a Negro; the family cut her out.
Had a cousin once.
Blackberries bloom only once,
bear fruit and then they die.
The only ripe color is black.

Grandfather, I've waited my whole white blossoming life
for one man to sow a seed,
and yes he's black.
Together we are a solid strong stalk,
one that can endure winters with thick wet snow,
that will bend us to the ground.
Twined together we will resist.

But Grandfather, I'd still like to feel your hand
against my cheek and sit together
watching the white flowers expand
beyond the limits
of taut skin.

Present

I'm here to unfurl upwards
from light and air and seed,
taking from invisible
to make visible.

In the brick road I sink down
to know I'm here and realize
I need to climb beyond myself
so there will be some light in those
I'm with.

From the dead I hear my direction:
 Follow your light, push upward.
 Mind matters but heart more—
 the soil of the soul.

The Monarch

A yellow-green upside down crown surrounds
And embraces the fat purple monarch,
Steadily reigning for three months.
In an instant the blackberry is overthrown.

We Belong to the Wind

forever yearning for moments
before the fruit falls,
grasping to take
what we could not.
We have no roots, no soil,
only remembering
and
remembering
desire.

My Husband

        I knew I couldn't call.
So, I listened, listened hard
and while you were screaming
silent in the cave I listened,
listened hard.
        Because you see
when you think you're all alone
you're not. I'm on the walls,
in the air, sparking with the fire
and between the rain.
        So tell me nothing new,
nothing old. Today in the market
a thief was killed. Today in the market
someone stole; he had a name,
an age, a size. But that doesn't matter
now. The trees are stomping
high up into their black tufts.
        And you are rolling
over and over, over and over.
It's o.k. Time passes anyhow.
The branches stretch and bend
and somethings crack, let go
        But it's all there—
the cave, the fire
        and the echo.

Dissemination, Dispersal

One flower stands thigh high
as wide as my head.
How to scatter, send it off?
I take my hands over my eyes,
self-communion, reception
of breath. A sapling stands
whittled in the Eastern corner.
Do not cry. This is where the rope
will descend.

Can you hold it in a whole breath?

Cantering under moons I was
returned to a rocking, a tempering.
I opened my arms to warm
by the fire, to unroll the giant stamen
and breathe. My breath launched
each and every seed into the field.

Inside an Italian Kiss, Baci di Perugia

You can doubt the stars
have fire, but do not doubt my love.
I know you doubt my love, my sincerity.
I left you and you doubt.
But on this earth you return to me again and again.
I listen for your reverberation in the lightening.
I stand strong, feel the blows' weight and know
this strong tone is really a low, deep moan--
your desolation and despair manifested in air.
You can doubt the stars have fire,
but do not doubt my love.
I hear your heart's breath in the wind's swill,
lifting my hair: *come back for me, reviens pour moi,*
said years ago as if you knew those words would return
here to this earth.

REFERENCES/NOTES

Poem titles, page number, then reference or note.

Invisible Offerings [page 3]:

The phrase "lovers propose but God dispenses" is from the French phrase "on propose, mais Dieu dispose." Balafon is a xylophone.

Fully Colored Green [page 9]:

This was inspired by the mineral world in Larissa Szporluk's collection *Embryos and Idiots*.

Bleached History [page 11]:

This poem was inspired by Burkinabe shaman Malidome Patrice Somé's autobiography, *Of Water and Spirit*. Somé was kidnapped as a young child by missionaries and taken to missionary school; he escaped in his late teens, returning to his village. In the 1950s children were punished if they spoke their native languages at school; French was the language of instruction in Burkina Faso. *Dolo* is homemade grain alcohol. Calabash is a gourd. Calabash are dried and used as bowls, among other things. Wearing an antelope skull signifies shame, akin to wearing a dunce cap. Narelwindé, Awa and Yalle are Burkinabe first names. Baobab is a tree of utmost significance to West Africa, signifying strength and groundedness.

In My blood I Carry You [page 13]:

Potica is a nut roll dessert, *krofe* are donuts, *flancate* is a fried sweet dough, cut in rectangles.

Scratching Back [page 16]:

The Harmattan is a dry wind scattering soil in West Africa. *Griot* is a praise singer, a keeper of history.

Fierce Love [Page 23]:

Tamtams is French for drums

Compulsion [page 25]:

Babushka means grandma

Ascension [page 30]:

This poem incorporates phrases from the *Mooré* language, which is from the Mossi ethnicity in Burkina Faso; about five million people speak it. The Mossi are the dominant ethnicity in Burkina. "Mam yeeta Kongossi" means I am from Kongoussi; Kongoussi is a town in Burkina Faso. "Mam yoor la Narelwindé" means My name is Narelwindé. Wuro is the god of creation from the Bobo ethnicitiy in Burkina Faso.

From Africa to Russia [page 40]:

Pelmeni are like tortellini but filled with meat. *Vatrushka* are circular pastry with a cheese filling. *Pirozhki* are small pockets of dough filled with many different fillings, such as mushrooms, cabbage or meat. Cowrie shells were currency centuries ago in much of Africa. They were highly prized. They also are used for divinations.

Let's Go Green [page 48]:

The Duomo refers to the church in Florence, Italy.

It's Hard to Embrace Betrayal [page 71]:

Takes place in Ouidah, Benin. Ouidah was a central port in the slave route. There is a newly constructed memorial called the Point of no return. The Portuguese fort was built in 1721. King Agadja of Dhomey planted a tree at the Grande Place de Zoungbodji where slaves would circle it three times to ensure their spirits return.

Blackberry Babies [pages 79]:

An illegitimate child; also blackberry patch baby; Arkansas, 1907, from Harold Wentworth's *American Dialect Dictionary*, 1944

Controlling Sacrifices [pages 80]:

This is an entirely imagined ceremony, not based on anything real. Loba was a deity I created.

Because Bones are Solid, Permanent [page 89]:

This poem was inspired by Burkinabe shaman (woman) Sobonfu Somé's book *The Spirit of Intimacy: Ancient Teachings in the Ways of Relationships*. She mentions some healing ceremonies that a community helps to carry out to heal couples.

Answering [page 95]:

"Je veux que tu restes avec moi" means "I want you to stay with me." "Offerings at the crossroads" refers to indigenous religious practice of putting food out to gods where roads intersect, asking for blessings.

"Viens, Viens, Viens Chez Moi" [page 98]:

The title means come, come, come to me. "Tes fesses sont comme le mur" means your buns are like the wall.

Inside an Italian Kiss, Baci di Perugia [page 115]:

This is based off the Italian chocolate called Baci, Italian for kisses. Inside each candy there is a romantic saying.

PREVIOUS PUBLISHING CREDITS

Acknowledgment is made to the following publications where these poems, some in earlier versions, first appeared:

Colere: "Self Possession," and "Clarification."

Frigg: "Seven Yesterdays and Todays," "On Stage," "Scratching Back," "A Significant Reason," "Fruit Withheld," "Fully Colored Green," "A Single Breath," and "Self Possession."

Jenda: A Journal of Culture and African Women Studies: "Because Bones are Solid, Permanent."

Little Red Tree International Poetry Prize Anthology 2013: "Inch by Inch Row by Row."

Long River Review: "Working for an NGO in Allada, Benin," and "FruitLove."

Nazar Look: "Invisible Offerings," "FruitLove," "This Circular Space," and "I Carried You Before You Fully Came."

Poetic Journeys (public posters) University of Connecticut: "Answering."

Slab: "The Monarch."

Through a Distant Lens: Travel Poems: "From Africa to Russia."

INDEX

Poem titles are in bold and first lines in italic.

ABOUT THE AUTHOR

Suzanne Ondrus

Suzanne Ondrus is a poet whose work explores cultural identity and the human dramas that shape and transcend it. She holds an MFA in Poetry from Bowling Green State University; an MA in English from Binghamton SUNY; BA from Wells College and presently is completing her doctoral dissertation on African women's epistolaries through the University of Connecticut. Born in Ohio, her experiences living in Benin, Burkina Faso, Uganda, Russia, Italy, and Germany shape her artistic vision. She is fluent in Italian, French, and German. Her poems have appeared in *Reed Magazine*, *Slab*, *Contemporary Verse 2*, *Colere*, and *The Long River Review*.

Suzanne is the winner of the third *Vernice Quebodeaux "Pathways" Poetry Prize for Poetry*, leading to the publication by Little Red Tree Publishing of this book of poetry, *Passion Seeds*.